STRAWBERRY HILL
Renaissance Glass

MICHAEL PEOVER

SCALA

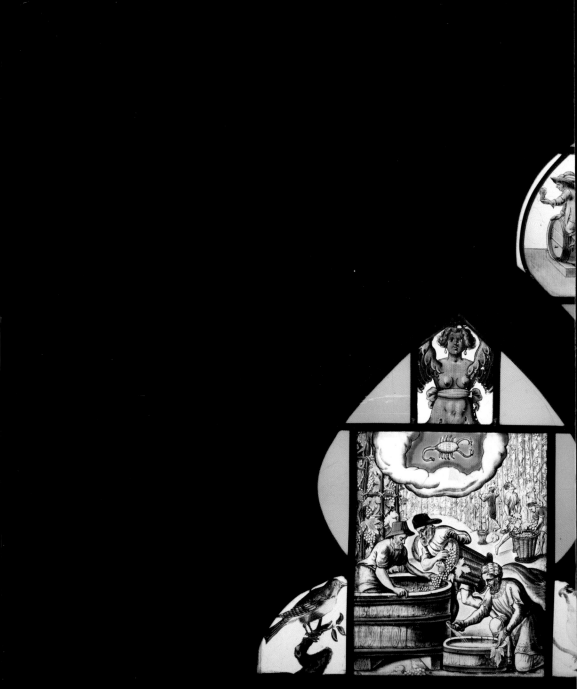

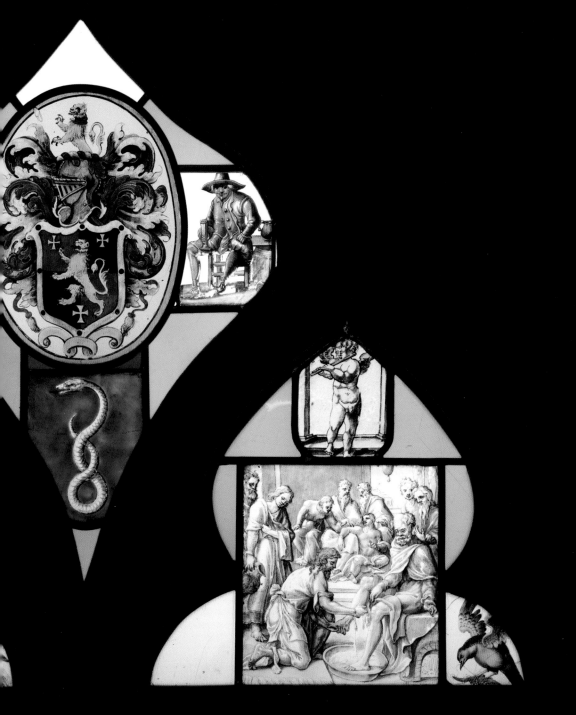

INTRODUCTION

ABOVE
A Bird with a Large Insect (Bee-eater?),
17th century
95 x 75 mm
Little Parlour

OPPOSITE
A Colourful Bird, 17th century
95 x 75 mm
Little Parlour

Horace Walpole (1717–1797) bought a modest house in 1748 and spent the rest of his life remodelling and extending it to form his little gothic castle, Strawberry Hill. In 1753, he wrote:

> I have carpenters to direct, plasterers to hurry, papermen to scold, and glaziers to help: this last is my greatest pleasure: I have amassed such quantities of painted glass, that every window in my castle will be illuminated with it: the adjusting and disposing it is vast amusement. (Letter to Horace Mann, 27 April 1753.)

Walpole also described how he had obtained most of his painted glass in 1750 from

> One Asciotti, an Italian, who had married a Fleming … . I sent him to Flanders and he brought me 450 pieces, for which and his journey I paid him 36 guineas … . All this manufacture consisted entirely in rounds of scripture stories, stained in black and yellow, or in small figures in black and white, birds and flowers in colour, and Dutch and Flemish arms. (*Book of Materials*, 1759, p.71.)

Walpole's Flemish glass would have been intended for the rectangular windows formed by simple frames; but he wished to use it in his gothic windows with their arched tops and cusped shapes. Moreover, the painted glass was confined to these shaped tops in most of the windows, allowing clear views through the lower panes across his gardens and distant prospects; it is only in a few locations such as those in the Armoury and Hall where the entire window is filled, there being no interesting view to be had from there. With his architect, John Chute (1701–1776), Walpole must have devised the window tracery to accommodate a single roundel between the points of the cusps, filling in the remaining spaces with small figures, birds, flowers and so on, rather in the way quarries, or small panes of glass, were used in medieval windows. Even when he introduced rectangular windows, as in the Great Parlour, he inserted lancet-shaped frames to preserve the gothic presentation.

The glass that Walpole imported is much older than his house, dating from about 1540–1660 and created by glass painters in the Low Countries (now the Netherlands and parts of Belgium). The advent of the Reformation in the 1520s, together with changes in architectural style, had reduced the market for large windows of stained and painted glass in ecclesiastical settings. But the growing prosperity and remarkable flowering of interest in the arts in the Netherlands at this time provided the glass painters with opportunities to create small panels of painted glass for domestic situations – merchants' houses, shops, almshouses, hospitals, town halls; these panels are commonly termed 'roundels' whatever their shape. The designs used for roundels were often based on the work of popular contemporary artists; at Strawberry Hill many of the designs can be traced to the work of the painter Maarten van Heemskerck (1498–1574), among others, who worked at Haarlem and was active from 1527 to his death in 1574. In England, paintings by Heemskerck can be seen at the National Gallery, London, the Fitzwilliam Museum, Cambridge, and at Hampton Court Palace. The popularity and availability of prints of artists' work at this time provided the glass painters with ready-made designs from which to make their roundels. In the early sixteenth century, the roundels were executed in shades of black and brown paint enlivened with details in yellow or orange stain, but in the latter half of the century coloured enamel paints were increasingly used.

The subject matter chosen for this domestic glass was commonly based on biblical stories; in the Protestant north, both New and Old Testament scenes, while in the south – the Spanish Netherlands – scenes from the New Testament and the lives of the Saints predominate. While Walpole did not reveal where in Flanders his agent Asciotti had obtained his 'immense cargo' of painted glass, the subject matter suggests it was principally from the north of the region, that is, the modern-day Netherlands. In addition to biblical scenes, secular scenes drawn from everyday life were popular, such as hunting, fishing and farming activities. Often there were sequences containing activities illustrating, for example, Labours of the Months or The Seasons. Other popular subjects were flowers and birds, animals, fish and

insects, and these were originally intended to form parts of the decorative surround to a central roundel; exotic varieties were favoured as reminders of the trophies of overseas trade. The 'small figures in black and white' to which Walpole refers include peasants engaged in dancing or drinking as well as cavaliers and fine ladies, all providing a celebration of the life that prosperity had brought to the region. Walpole liked particularly the colourful Dutch and Flemish armorials of which he writes 'I call them the achievements of the old Counts of Strawberry' (Letter to Horace Mann, 18 October 1750).

His wish to create a sense of English history in an ancient house was further strengthened by mixing the armorials and heraldic devices in stained glass of noble English families with his Flemish roundels. Sadly, much of the English glass is now lost. But the armorial glass celebrating his own family, and created 'on purpose' for him in 1761 and 1772 by the York glass painter William Peckitt (bap. 1731–d.1795), survives in the Great North Bedchamber and has been recreated in the Long Gallery from contemporary descriptions and watercolours. This new work that he commissioned employs a rich

palette of coloured glass surrounding the main panels, imitating medieval 'mosaic'. An important aspect of Walpole's use of glass is that of colour. Although the glaziers he employed earlier were of varying proficiency, the plain-coloured glass that they used to surround his old glass demonstrates his preoccupation with what he considered to be an appropriate setting, as was later realised for him by Peckitt. He could then write of his house 'the conventual gloom of the inside, which however, when the sun shines, is gorgeous, as he appears all crimson and gold and azure through the painted glass' (Letter to Horace Mann, 30 September 1784).

Walpole's use of continental glass started a fashion among antiquarian collectors, with public auctions in 1761 and 1773 in London. The occupation of the Low Countries by the French in 1792 followed by the Napoleonic wars (1799–1814) released glass from monasteries across Germany and the Netherlands, much of which can now be found in English cathedrals, churches, stately homes and in museums here and in the USA. But nowhere is the glass integrated into the fabric of the building as at Strawberry Hill. Walpole even copied the designs for

chairs and based his knights on his Library ceiling on those in the Library windows.

Despite the ravages of time, war and losses in the 1842 great sale of the contents of Strawberry Hill, about half of the glass remains and can now be appreciated in the windows in the arrangements Walpole intended, creating effects of light, shade, colour and surprise as the visitor moves through the house.

ABOVE LEFT
An Exotic Bird Perching, 17th century
95 x 83 mm
China Closet

ABOVE RIGHT
A Swallow Perching, 17th century
95 x 83 mm
Little Parlour

Tolck twiften tegen mofe om water fij hem
moeijen
godt door mofe wt eenen Rotfteen water
Doet Vloeijen
Tobias ǯe Hem
) 6 1 2

Moses Striking the Rock in the Desert, dated 1612
210 x 160 mm
Great Parlour

This roundel has an inscription translated as 'The people quarrelled with Moses, they were worried about water. God through Moses makes water flow from a rock. Tobias de Hem 1612'. The design, and that of the companion piece in the same window *The Israelites Gathering Manna*, comes from drawings by Crispin van den Broeck (1523–1591) published as engravings in 1585. Moses stands in front of the rock with his stick raised and a stream of water gushes out; men and women queue with bowls, and the women give water to their parched children. Two camels, one drinking from the stream, are anatomically only approximate. The monogram above the scene is formed of the letters TDH; evidently this was from the name of the man who gave or commissioned the roundel in 1612. The scene is executed in sepia pigment, yellow stain being reserved for emphasising the surround and decorative scroll.

The Israelites Gathering Manna, dated 1612
280 x 215 mm
Great Parlour

The inscription on the roundel means 'The Children of Israel muttered greatly against Moses because they were starving but God fed them on heavenly bread. Josyna Loten 1612'. Men and women brush the manna into shallow bowls watched by Moses at the far left of the scene; this is a companion piece to *Moses Striking the Rock in the Desert* in the same window.

*Zebulon, c.*1600
175 x 270 mm
China Closet

One of the twelve sons of Jacob, Zebulon (inscribed Sebulon on the roundel) was one of twelve Patriarchs and an ancestor of the tribe of the same name. The design is after Maarten van Heemskerck (1498–1574) and another Patriarch by him, Gad, is in the same window. Both have needed considerable repainting, which has been copied from the original designs onto separate sheets of glass placed under the originals. Heemskerck has treated the subjects as classical heroes, but the glass painter has clothed the almost naked figure of Zebulon in a jerkin and trousers. He appears to be making or repairing a net that is being set up between posts. The meaning of the scene is obscure.

9

Noah and the Dove, c.1525
230 x 192 mm
Hall Lobby

The glass carrying this naive and charming depiction of Noah in the ark receiving the dove was badly corroded; expert cleaning revealed the shore and buildings in the background, which have been repainted on a separate sheet of glass placed under the original.

OPPOSITE
Jacob's Dream, c.1590
250 x 120 mm
Great Parlour

Jacob lies sleeping, propped against a tree trunk, dreaming of the ladder stretching to a bank of clouds with angels going up and down. In the biblical account, God spoke to Jacob from the cloud, promising the land to his descendants. The scene was drawn by Marten de Vos (1532–1603) and first published in 1585, but the glass painter has adapted it to fit the oval shape; an angel standing at the foot of the ladder and the face of God in the cloud have been omitted. Very skilled use of shading was required to differentiate the scene's elements.

The Procession of Haman,
*c.*1525
225 x 225 mm
Star Chamber

This finely painted roundel shows three scenes from the story of Haman and Mordecai in the Book of Esther. Haman was a minister in the King of Persia's court and Mordecai's niece Esther was the King's wife. Haman is seen, grandly dressed, riding his splendid steed in procession through the city accompanied by his groom who runs by his side and his dog that runs behind. On the far left, a man doffs his hat but Mordecai, sitting on the ground, refuses to respond. In the scene to the right, Haman is so incensed that he persuades the King to kill all Jews in the kingdom, not realising that this would mean the death of the King's wife. When Mordecai explains the consequences, the King invites them all to a dinner, seen in the room to the left, at which he denounces Haman and sentences him to the fate he wished for Mordecai.

Golden yellow stain is used sparingly on the foreground figures and to draw attention to the scene at the right. A small section is missing on the right, which may well have shown a gallows in Haman's garden, destined for Mordecai but where Haman himself is hanged.

OPPOSITE
*Nebuchadnezzar at Prayer, c.*1590
240 x 195 mm
Little Parlour

Nebuchadnezzar, the all-powerful ruler of Babylon, was attacked by madness for a period of seven years and at times lived like an animal; his sanity returned when he acknowledged God's supremacy. This scene portrays the moment when he has laid aside his crown and sceptre and gives thanks. His advisors and courtiers stand around with expressions of surprise and concern. This scene would have been intended to convey the importance of humbleness; it is based on a drawing by Lambert van Noort (1520–1571) in a series on Nebuchadnezzar and his dreams.

The glass painter has fashioned a wide variation of tone, with subtle highlights moulding the figures.

NEW TESTAMENT

Christ Washing the Disciple's Feet, c.1560
218 x 200 mm
Little Parlour

This beautifully drawn and shaded roundel is based on a design by Maarten van Heemskerck (1498–1574), dated 1548, which itself is strongly influenced by a woodcut by Albrecht Dürer (1471–1528) in his series 'The Small Passion' of 1511; Dürer had visited Antwerp, Bruges and Ghent in 1520 and his influence spread rapidly. Peter is seated on a bench, his feet over a bowl, and Christ kneels before him washing Peter's right foot. To the left, a disciple stands with a jug and a cloth. A flight of steps leads to the other disciples who sit or stand around watching. The glass painter has cropped the design to fit the space available and only nine disciples are shown; in the original design, the scene is set in a tall room with several hanging lamps, the base of one of which can be seen above Peter's head. Pale yellow stain is used to lighten the composition.

Releasing the Prisoner, c.1515
240 x 200 mm
Little Parlour

Releasing the Prisoner, from a series of the Acts of Mercy, is one of the earliest roundels in the house, of *c.*1515, as yet largely untouched by Renaissance influence. Christ is seen on the right-hand side, with a halo and his hand raised in blessing. The gaoler, with a key in his hand, approaches the seated and chained prisoner. In the background, a man sits in the stocks. Golden yellow stain is used to highlight beards, elements of the garments, the columns and to make the stocks more legible in the gloomy prison.

The Last Judgement, c.1590
235 x 205 mm
Great Parlour

This strongly modelled subject
is based on a Heemskerck design
but is very different in style from
Christ Washing the Disciple's Feet
(see p.15). Heemskerck had
visited Rome in 1532–35 and was
much influenced by the works of
Michelangelo (1475–1564) and
the Mannerists. The almost naked
and highly muscled Jew lies prone
across the horse, with much
foreshortening. The drawing of
the Samaritan and his horse is
full of movement; both turn their
heads as though distracted from
their course, the Samaritan's beard
streaming over his shoulder and
his upper body twisted. Dark
yellow stain is used on the horse's
trappings, elements of the
Samaritan's clothing and the
immediate foreground, which
thrusts the image forward. In the
far distance are figures going
about their business outside a
castellated town.

This version of the Last Judgement is based on a Heemskerck
design. God sits on a bank of clouds from which trumpets
protrude, sounding the last trump. The heads of cherubs poke
out from the cloud. In the foreground, two almost naked and
highly muscled men shield their eyes from the sight. To the left,
a devil pushes the damned to their fate, while to the right a
winged angel ushers the saved to heaven. This is the opposite of
the usual convention where the damned are to God's left and
may indicate that the roundel was copied from the original
drawing rather than a print of it, which would have reversed the
design. Much chiaroscuro, or heavy shading, is used to heighten
the drama and emphasise the different levels.

St Gregory the Great Writing, 17th century
220 x 220 mm
Library

St Peter and St Paul with the Sudarium, c.1525
210 mm diameter roundel
China Closet

The sudarium is the veil which, according to the Apocrypha, St Veronica placed over the face of Christ on his journey to Calvary to absorb perspiration and which retained an image of his face; it is preserved as a holy relic in St Peter's in Rome. Here it is held by St Peter and St Paul, patron saints of Rome. The tall, impressively impassive figures are bearded. St Peter holds the keys of Heaven and St Paul the large sword of martyrdom by which he was beheaded. Dark yellow stain is used for the haloes, including that of the image of Christ, the saint's attributes and borders of their voluminous robes, and the foreground. The bleak landscape supports some stylised plants and a barren tree.

The stern figures are typical of the School of Leiden at the early part of the sixteenth century. Unfortunately, the roundel has been cut down on all sides so that parts of the haloes, and St Paul's head and feet are now incomplete.

Gregory was one of the four fathers of the Church and this design is from a series of drawings of them by Marten de Vos (1532–1603), an Antwerp painter influenced by Venetian art who is believed to have spent time working with Tintoretto (1518–1594) in Venice. Here Gregory is seated, wearing the papal tiara and gown and holding his papal staff, a triple cross, while writing in a large book. On the table another book lies open, propped against a pile of books and on the table lie an inkwell, powder sprinkler and paper-knife. A small dog is curled up near his master's feet. At the end of the room is an open balustrade below which hangs a cardinal's red hat on a purple drape covering the wall; the tables are covered in purple cloth. On the chair back is embroidered the crest of six balls usually attributed to the Medici family, a reference to Gregory's continuing relevance to the modern world.

Walpole was very proud of his Library and must have spent much time there; no doubt when arranging his glass this subject would have seemed particularly appropriate there.

The Departure of the Prodigal Son, 1612
250 x 270 mm
Armoury

The parable of the prodigal son
was a very popular subject in the
art of the Renaissance in the
Low Countries. The son
asked for his patrimony to
seek his fortune. However,
he squandered the money
on drinking and whoring
and he was reduced to
becoming a swineherd
and sharing the pigs'
food in order to survive.
Eventually he returned
home asking for
forgiveness and was
welcomed back into
the family. For the
newly affluent in a
country benefiting from
expanding overseas trade,
this was seen as a salutary
tale. Artists produced
sequences of scenes from the
story, which were engraved
and made into prints. The
example here is from such
a series of 1562 by Heemskerck.
The son is on his horse, turning
in the saddle to wave farewell
to his father, while his mother
watches in the background.
The inscription is translated as
'The Prodigal Son thoughtlessly
demanded his inheritance from
his mother 1612'. The glass
painter was evidently still using
Heemskerck's design 50 years
after its publication.
    This roundel has suffered
from loss of paint over the years,
but the images are still legible.

ALL THE MAJOR representations of ancient classical subjects at Strawberry Hill are to be found in the Great Parlour, perhaps accounted for by an association of learning with meals in hall, which Walpole would have experienced at King's College Cambridge.

A Classical Group, 16th century
200 x 290 mm
Great Parlour

This strange group of figures, called *Heathen Deities* for the 1842 great sale, fortunately have their names written next to them. Sitting on the left with his back to a classical column is Vulcan (VULCANUS), god of Fire, holding tongs and a hammer, which he used for forging; above him flies the naked figure of Aeolus (ÆOLUS), god of Wind, blowing vigorously. Around the fire sit Somnus (SUMNUS), sleep or laziness, then FRIGUS, for cold, shown as a man warming his hands at the fire. In the background are

Poverty (PAUPERUS) holding her begging basket, and nearby Rebellion (DEFECTUS) makes off with her arms folded. Closer to the fire is Darkness (TENEBRAE) holding her lamp. In the fore-ground is written Anacharsis (ANACHARSES), a Scythian philosopher with the reputation of observing Greek life; presumably he is the figure by the fire in side view, perhaps writing. Above them all is a cloud on which can be seen a glimpse of another figure, the top of which has been removed. Yellow stain is used sparingly, for the flames, for the begging basket and hat of Poverty and the belt of Darkness. No design for this enigmatic scene has been found.

The Triumph of Fame,
16th century
190 x 305 mm
Great Parlour

There are two remarkable versions
of the *Triumph of Fame* and the
Triumph of Time that are very
unusual in presenting the
perspective for the chariots
from the front instead of the
usual side view.

Fame is named FAMA
and his chariot is drawn by
two elephants. On Fame's
right stand men of letters
carrying books and named
CATO, CICERO and
HOMERUS, and on his
left are men of action,
HECTOR, HANNIBAL
and HERCULES with
pike, sword and club
respectively. From the
chariot hangs a human
skull below which is written
MORS (death) and an
emaciated man holding a
long pole lies in its path,
reminders of the transient
nature of fame. Walpole
described this roundel in his
1784 'Description' of the house
as 'a Dutch piece representing the
Triumph of Fame, who is
accompanied by Cato, Cicero, and
other great men in square caps
and gowns of masters of Arts.'

The Triumph of Time,
16th century
190 x 300 mm
Great Parlour

Time, TEMPUS, is represented
as a bearded man holding an
hourglass and a clock with a bell;
he rides in a chariot drawn by
stags. On the ground, littered
with discarded books and
weapons, lies Fame with
her chariot in pieces.
The background shows
the ruins of a great city
named TROEIEN (Troy).
On an open book on which
a stag is stepping
is written Laurentiens,
possibly a reference to
the Laurentian Library
in Florence, and Talesins.
The latter is usually
written Taliesin and is the
name of a sixth-century
Welsh bard known for his
accounts of the labours of
Hercules in the vernacular
and which legend says was
in the court of King Arthur,
but surely a surprising
reference in a sixteenth-century
roundel of Netherlands origin.

EMPVS

TROIEN·

Laurencius Galesius

25

The Samian Sybil, 17th century
135 x 100 mm
Library

The Sybils were ancient prophetesses, of
which there were twelve, who foretold the
future at the Oracle of Delphi. The design
is by Crispin van de Passe the Elder
(*c.*1564–1637) in the form of a portrait
miniature. Here, with a book in her right
hand and clutching a crown of thorns
the Sybil is represented as foretelling the
Christian story in much the same way
as Old Testament scenes were sometimes
used to prefigure events in the New
Testament. She wears a grand hat tied
with ribbons over her dark brown hair and
a mulberry robe over her dress. Her name
is written on the yellow rim of the roundel.

A Winged Female Harpy,
16th century
95 x 70 mm
Little Parlour

In Greek mythology, harpies were
monsters that were a combination
of human and animal shapes.
This lively piece shows a harpy
with raised winged arms, wearing
earrings and a sash about her
waist. She commonly represents
avarice, one of the seven deadly
sins, in moral allegories.

The Wheel of Fortune, dated 1660
210 x 160 mm
Great Parlour

A phoenix holds the wheel with a foot and its beak. A man balances on top of the wheel and above his head is written Carel de II. A man makes vain attempts to clamber up on one side of the wheel and another is tumbling off on the other side, his blue cloak flying around him. A bleeding man lies prostrate under the wheel where is written Cromwel. The date 1660 is written in the lower panel but the rest of the inscription is now indecipherable. Walpole mentioned this roundel in his 1784 'Description' of the house: 'there is another Dutch emblematic piece, which is Charles 2nd riding uppermost in the Wheel of Fortune, and Rebellion thrown down'.

Two of the Five Senses: Sight and Smell, 17th century
Each 110 x 80 mm
Beauty Room

The senses were a popular subject in Netherlandish art, particularly in engravings. A woman sits beneath a tree; sight is represented by a looking glass in which her face is reflected, while in the other roundel she holds and smells flowers. A bird with outstretched wings accompanies her for 'sight', while a charming lapdog gazes at her in 'smell'. Two other scenes in the same series are in the Red Bedchamber and represent 'hearing', a woman with a stringed guitar and a seated stag, and 'taste', where a woman samples a bowl of fruit.

PREVIOUS PAGE
Winter – the Frozen River,
17th century
220 x 160 mm
Great Parlour

This version of Winter has a
young man surveying the scene
on a frozen river outside a city
whose buildings and towers loom
in the background. He is blowing
on his hands to warm them and
has a stick on his shoulder,
possibly to break a hole in the ice
to fish through. Several incidents
are shown on the ice: an old
woman has toppled on her skates,
her skirt over her head; a woman
with a child in a basket; a man
pushing barrels on a sled; others
walking about carrying sticks
and one fishing through a hole in
the ice. The caption below the
splendid grotesque head can be
translated: 'Although the golden
sun comes to peep through a
crack/The hard frost has not
forgotten its cold. You'd best stay
awhile in the fold, I consider that
the best/It's all too early to fly out
of the nest'.

ABOVE
Autumn – Picking Apples,
17th century
270 x 210 mm
Star Chamber

Titled 'September', this scene
shows a man laden with apples
surveying the field in which a
team of apple pickers go about
their work. Ladders and fallen
apples and pears litter the ground
around him. Another man climbs
a ladder while others fill tall
baskets. In the distance, men are
carrying baskets to a large town,
the outline of which can be seen
on the skyline.

OPPOSITE
Autumn – Pressing the Grapes,
*c.*1550
235 x 195 mm
Little Parlour

The use of grapes or vine leaves
as symbols of Autumn goes back
to Roman frescos. In this lively
version, a man is treading the
grapes in a large tub while another
adds more fruit from a basket and
the juice is run off to a shallow
tub. To the side are vines heavy
with grapes yet to be picked and
in the background men fill more
baskets from rows of tall vines.

Summer – Harvesting,
17th century
210 x 160 mm
Great Parlour

Summer is traditionally
associated with the sickle
and sheaves of corn, as
seen in this roundel
where a woman, in the
shade of a tree, pauses
in her work to talk with
a man who is himself
laden with fruit. In her
hat she wears ears of
corn. Further off is a field
with uncut corn and men
and women continue the
work and build a haystack on
higher ground. Farm buildings
lie in the background.

Winter – Fisherwoman,
17th century
215 x 160 mm
Great Parlour

Another version of
Winter, also in the Great
Parlour, has an old man,
well muffled against the
cold, who is buying fish
from a wooden box tied
around a woman's waist
and over a blue apron.
On the ice are two horse-
drawn sleds and men
carrying sticks, some with
their dogs. In the distance
is a castle. The inscription
can be translated as: 'The winter
has its pleasures. Come onto the
ice, but best on all fours'.

Winter – an Old Man, c.1600
275 x 125 mm
Star Chamber

Winter is often associated with an
old man thickly clad and wrapped
in a cloak. Here, his cloak is
trimmed with fur and he warms
his hands with a pot of steaming
coals. To the right, men are
carrying bundles of firewood from
the bare trees, outlined against the
sky, and which they are felling.
To the left, two young couples
skate on the ice outside the walls
of a large city. In the sky the cold
wind blows strongly on the scene
and is personified by a puffing
head. Signs of the Zodiac are in
the sky where Hyems (winter) is
written. The wintry sky and
snow-covered ground complete
the desolation of the scene. The
old man's dark green hood and
sleeve are the only splashes of
colour other than the sparing use
of yellow stain. This arresting
scene is based on the design by
Hendrick Goltzius (1558–1617),
who was working in Haarlem
around 1580.

33

Hunting with Dogs,
17th century
90 x 90 mm
Little Parlour

This lively scene shows a fox about to be set upon by two hunting dogs, one of which has the fox by the tail. The huntsman is reining-in his horse for the kill and is wielding a sword; the splendid horse rears, his long curly mane flowing. In the background are high barren hills.

Hunting with a Falcon,
17th century
90 x 90 mm
Little Parlour

The huntsman, in a flowing tunic, strides away into the verdant landscape; he has a falcon on his right wrist and carries the leash attached to the retriever in his left hand. This time, in the foreground, the fox sits nonchalantly watching the departing group.

GENRE FIGURES

Subjects from everyday life became very popular in the seventeenth century, stemming from the decline in religious and decorative paintings and the increasing affluence of the general population. These studies did not represent idealised scenes but celebrated life at all levels of society, focusing particularly on peasants enjoying leisure time. The examples in the windows at Strawberry Hill created by glass painters are mainly of single figures and complemented the many paintings of Dutch and Flemish inn scenes and country life that hung on the walls in the house.

A Cavalier Holding a Rose,
17th century
113 x 80 mm
Great Parlour

The man is wearing his best clothes: a lace collar, a tassel and voluminous cloak. Holding his gloves in one hand, he proffers the rose with the other. Who is he wooing?

A Clerk Carrying a Scroll with a Red Seal,
17th century
110 x 88 mm
Great Parlour

The clerk wears a cloak and bows on his shoes.

OPPOSITE
A Dutch Burgher, 17th century
220 x 175 mm
Library

This was probably made for presentation to a civic worthy appointed to a prominent position in the local town. He is dressed in his parade regalia – fine breeches tied with bows, a plumed hat and a silk sash with tasselled ends across his jerkin – and carries a pike. His armorial or those of his peer group (crossed arrows) is displayed in a shield.

A Peasant Dancing and Drinking, 17th century
115 x 77 mm
Beauty Room

This lively figure is dressed in simple and rather dishevelled clothes and a furry hat; he holds a raised glass and a clay pipe; a knife hangs from his belt.

A Girl Dancing, 17th century
112 x 81 mm
Beauty Room

The girl wears a simple bonnet and a plain dress, but she has a necklace and her shoes are well polished. From her waist hangs a rope bearing a set of keys. Perhaps she was a ladies' maid with some free time.

A Fine Lady Dancing and Playing a Lute, 17th century
130 x 100 mm
Great Parlour

The lady wears a voluminous dress and fine shoes; in the background is an amorous couple. The inscription means 'As the saying goes, like mistress like servant'.

't gaet gelijck het Spreecwoort seijt,
so de Juffrou soo de meijt.

An Old Man Seated Holding a Tankard, 17th century
130 x 170 mm
Little Parlour

The man looks out at us as he sits on a table supported by a barrel and a stool; there is a jug beside him. He has undone his jerkin and his shirt spills out.

A Drinks Seller,
17th century
110 x 75 mm
Little Parlour

The seller's wooden tray of drinks bottles is held in place by straps round his neck and back and is propped up on a stick; he offers a cup in his hand.

A Reveller Drinking Astride a Barrel, 17th century
130 x 170 mm
Little Parlour

The man holds a large tankard. Despite his plumed hat and leather boots he looks the worse for drink.

A Peasant Playing a Hurdy-gurdy, 17th century
113 x 80 mm
Beauty Room

A heavily-built man, the peasant wears ragged breeches and worn shoes but has a fur-trimmed hat and a cloak thrown over his shirt. The hurdy-gurdy is tucked under his left arm and he plays it with his right hand.

An Elderly Couple Nursing a Baby, 17th century
100 x 90 mm
Library

This charming scene shows a seated couple, with the woman cradling a baby wrapped in swaddling clothes. They both look at the child tenderly and with concern. Are they the grandparents?

A Gentleman Playing a Side Drum, 17th century
115 x 85 mm
Great Parlour

The young gentleman wears a plumed hat and well-cut clothes. This may be a presentation piece to a member of a local military group – for example, as in *The Night Watch* (1642, Rijksmuseum Amsterdam) by Rembrandt (1606–1669).

A Man Dowsing?, 17th century
110 x 80 mm
Beauty Room

This enigmatic piece shows a
man dressed in slashed breeches
and jerkin with a cloak thrown
over his shoulder; his broad hat
carries a loop in which is fixed a
long-handled spoon. From his
leather shoulder-belt hangs a
knife or dagger and in his hand
is a two-pronged fork. Could this
be a dowsing fork?

*Arms of Ayliffe by
William Price,
c.*1690
280 x 200 mm
Little Parlour

Some English glass painters were active in the sixteenth and seventeenth centuries and produced panels, confined mainly to armorials, although their output was small in contrast to the large number of figurative scenes produced by their continental rivals. In the Great North Bedchamber Closet are the royal arms in a panel dated 1558, the year of Queen Elizabeth I's (1533–1603) accession to the throne, painted with great flair and delicacy and including a tiny St George with the dragon below the shield. The Little Parlour has the arms of the Ayliffe family, painted in a manner typical of the London glass painter William Price (*c*.1644–1710) around 1690 and comparable in quality to the continental glass. Price's grandson, William Price the Younger (1707–1765), was later employed by Walpole to paint

the Walpole family quarterings for the over-door to that room, and to set up the windows in the Tribune with old and new glass, much of which is lost.

Having exhausted his stock of continental and English glass by the 1760s, Walpole employed William Peckitt (1731–1795), from York, to paint armorials for the Long Gallery and Great North Bedchamber windows. The complete original set of the latter survive. The formulation of several of the coloured enamel paints was patented by Peckitt with an eye to the growing market for stained and painted glass. When the Great Parlour windows were altered in 1774, Walpole employed an Irish glass painter, James Pearson (*c*.1750–1838), who left a charming signed memento of his work, a cobbler whistling to a bird in a cage.

Shield of Intermarriage of Walpole and Cavendish by William Peckitt, 1771
200 x 150 mm
Great North Bedchamber

A Cobbler Whistling to a Bird in a Cage by James Pearson, 1774
270 x 290 mm
Great Parlour

Royal Armorial, dated 1558
240 x 180 mm
Great North Bedchamber Closet

DIEV · ET · MON · DROIT ·

A · D · 1558 ·

© Scala Publishers Ltd, 2010
Text © The Strawberry Hill Trust
Artworks © The Strawberry Hill Trust

Photographs
Front cover flap: © The Strawberry Hill Trust;
pp.4–17, 19–21, 24–31, 32 (top), 33–45, 46 (left):
© Paul San Casciani; pp.18, 32 (bottom), 46 (right):
© Chapel Studio; front cover, inside front cover,
back cover, inside back cover and pp.2–3, 22–23, 47:
© Martin Charles.

First published in 2010 by
Scala Publishers Ltd
Northburgh House
10 Northburgh Street
London EC1V 0AT
Telephone: +44 (0) 20 7490 9900
www.scalapublishers.com

In association with The Strawberry Hill Trust
www.friendsofstrawberryhill.org.uk and
www.strawberryhillhouse.org
Registered Charity No.: 1095618

ISBN: 978 1 85759 656 4

Project Manager and Copy Editor: Linda Schofield
Designer: Trevor Wilson Design Ltd
Printed and bound in China

10 9 8 7 6 5 4 3 2 1

British Library Cataloguing in Publication Data.
A catalogue record for this book is available from the
British Library.

Front cover:
Winter – the Frozen River (detail) (see p.30)
Front cover flap:
Strawberry Hill from the south-east, mid-1780s,
watercolour. © The Strawberry Hill Trust
Inside front cover:
A Classical Group (detail) (see p.21)
Frontispiece:
A Little Parlour window, first glazed about 1753,
with an eclectic mixture of sacred, profane and
heraldic subjects from *c*.1560–*c*.1690
Inside back cover:
Hunting with Dogs (detail) (see p.35)
Back cover:
A Cobbler Whistling to a Bird in a Cage by James Pearson
(detail) (see p.46)

ACKNOWLEDGEMENTS
The Strawberry Hill glass has been restored by
Chapel Studio, Stained Glass Ltd. Historical research
by Michael Peover, and Kevin Rogers of Inskip and
Jenkins, architects. The glass restoration was funded
by The Country Houses Foundation and a number
of donors to the Glass Preservation Fund. Translations
of the inscriptions provided by Paul Sharpling.